# PRINCIPAL COLORING BOOK FOR ADULTS

For free printable bonuses, please visit: **amyjandrews.com**

Copyright © 2021 by Amy J. Andrews
All rights reserved.

No part of this book may be reproduced in any form
or by any electronic or mechanical means,
including information storage and retrieval systems,
without written permission from the author.

## A Special Request

Your brief Amazon review could help us and also help other people find this book and receive the same benefit you have.

This link will take you to the Amazon.com review page for this book:

### amyjandrews.com/review12

Thank you for your support!

# ENJOY YOUR JOURNEY!

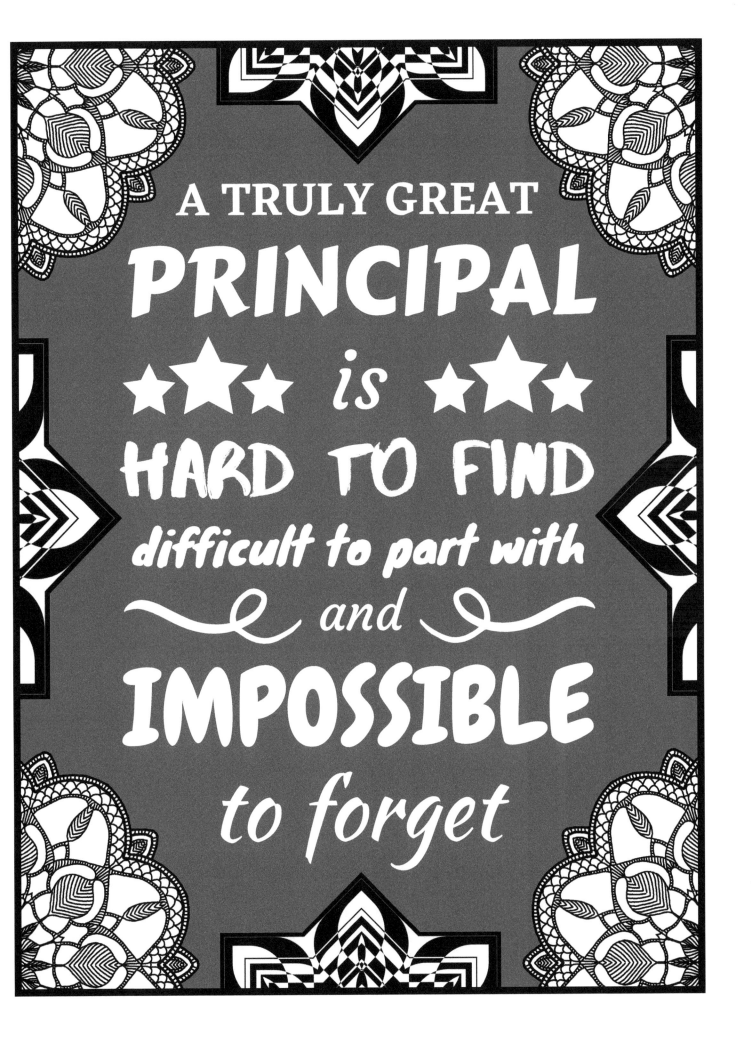

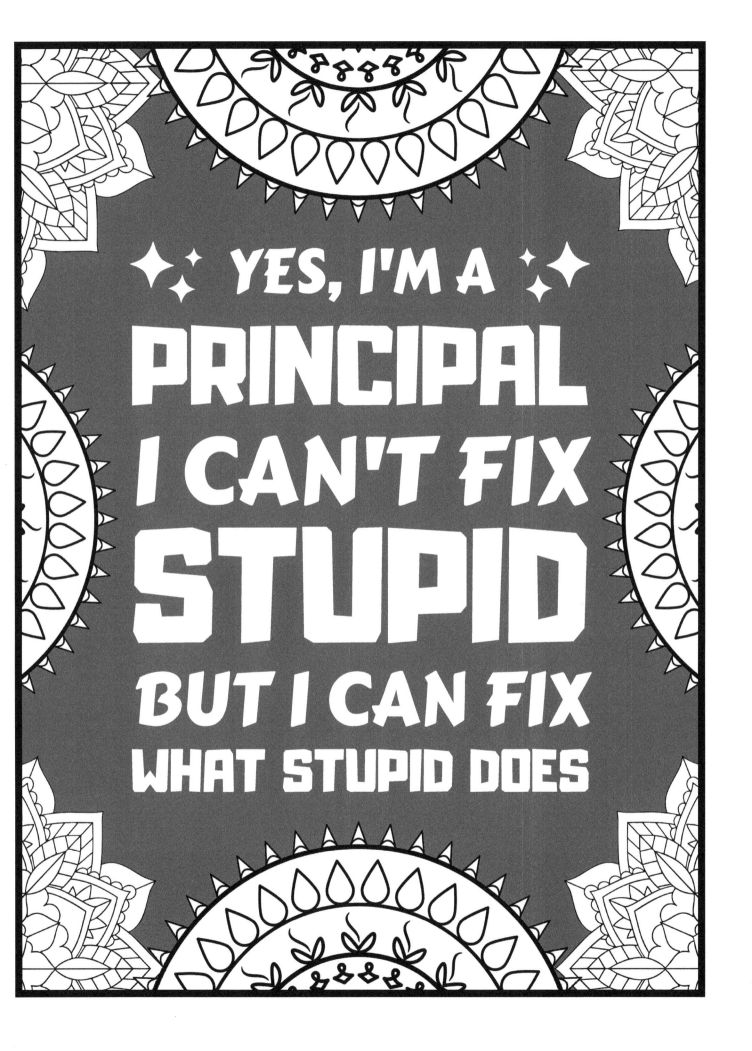

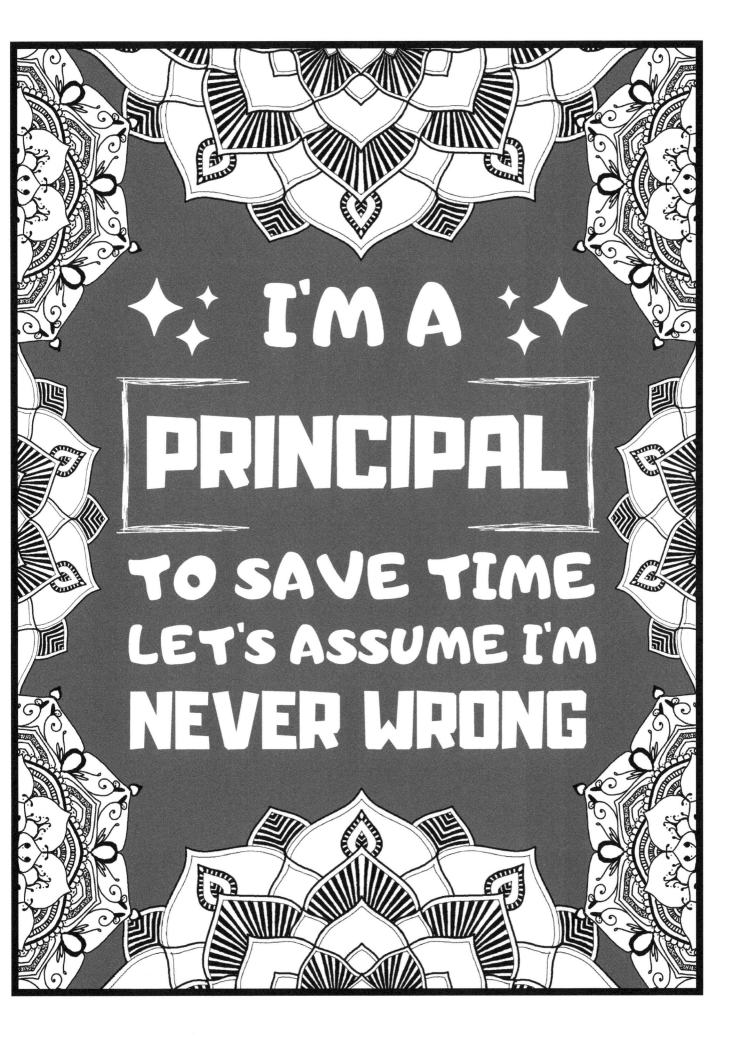

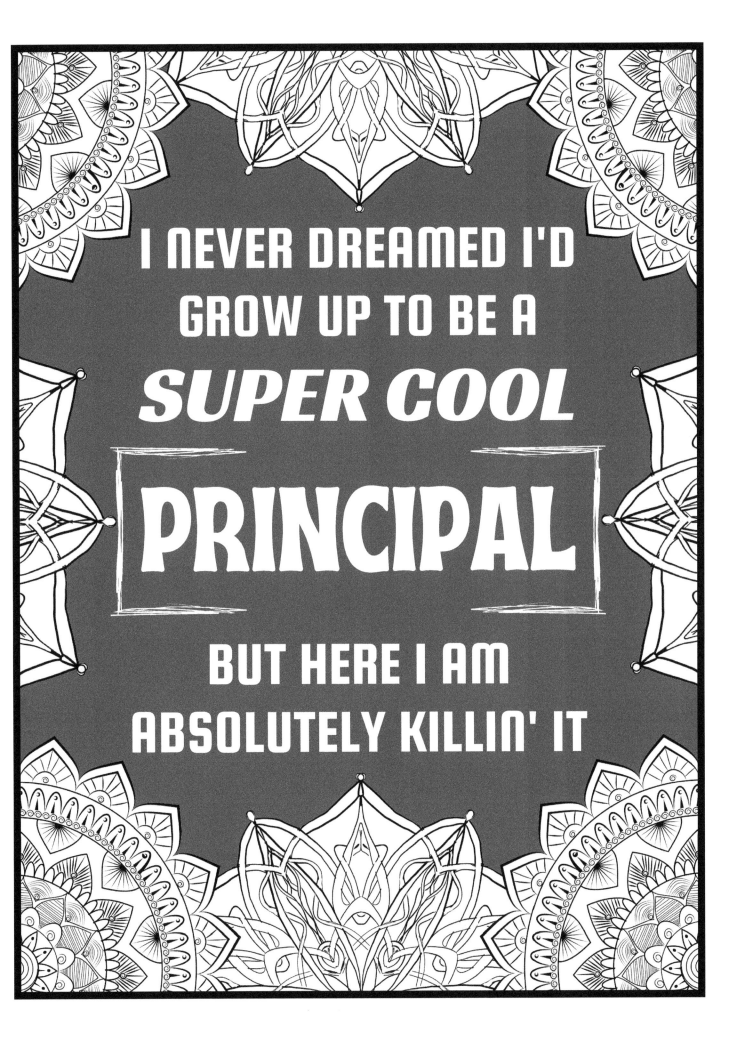

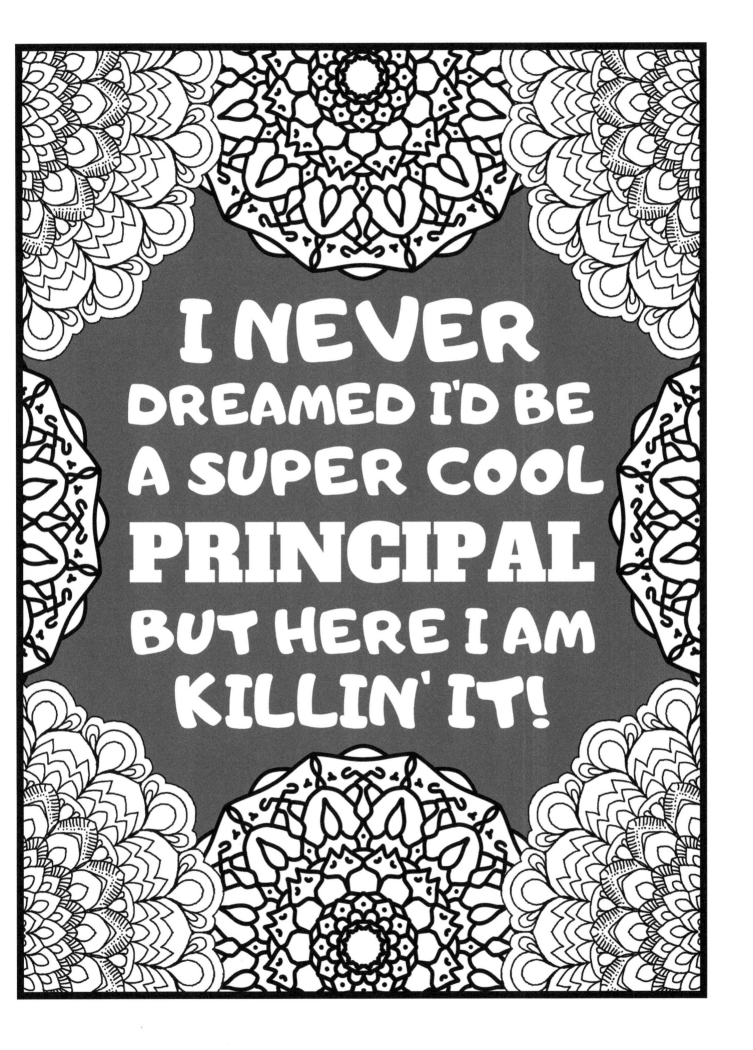

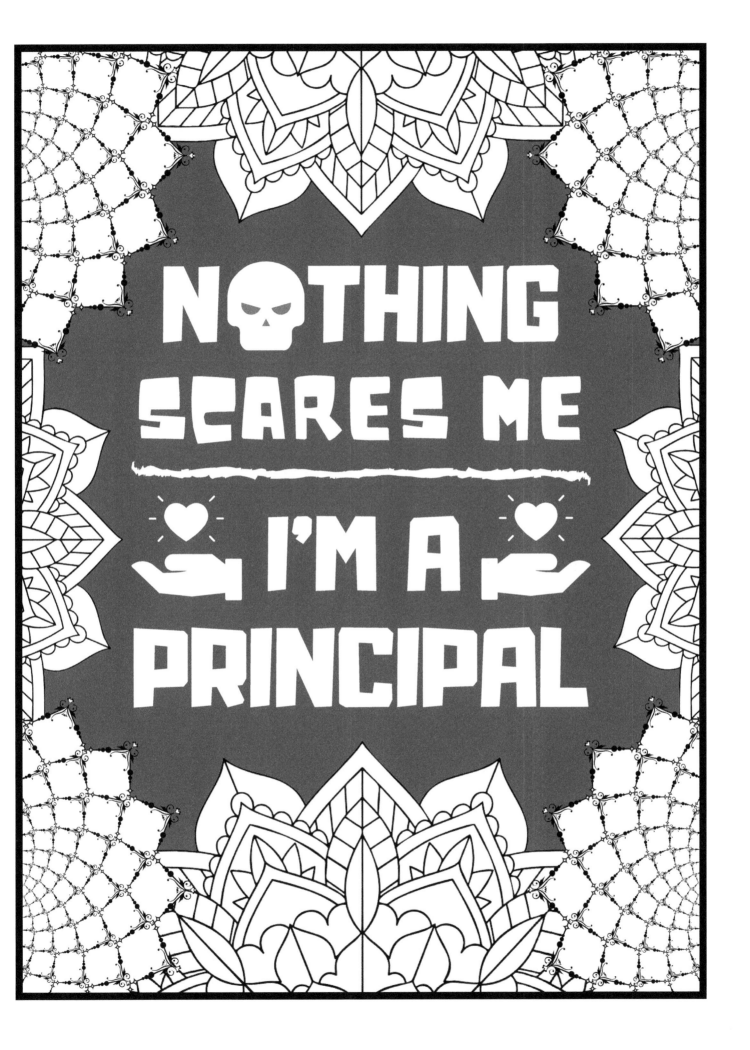

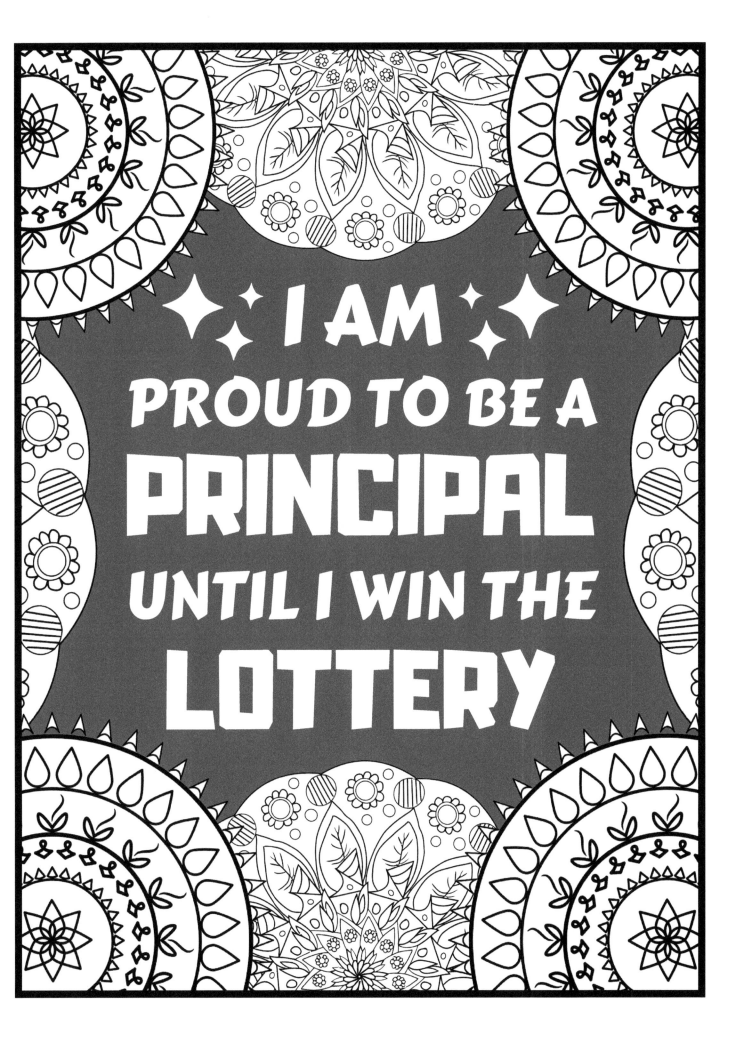

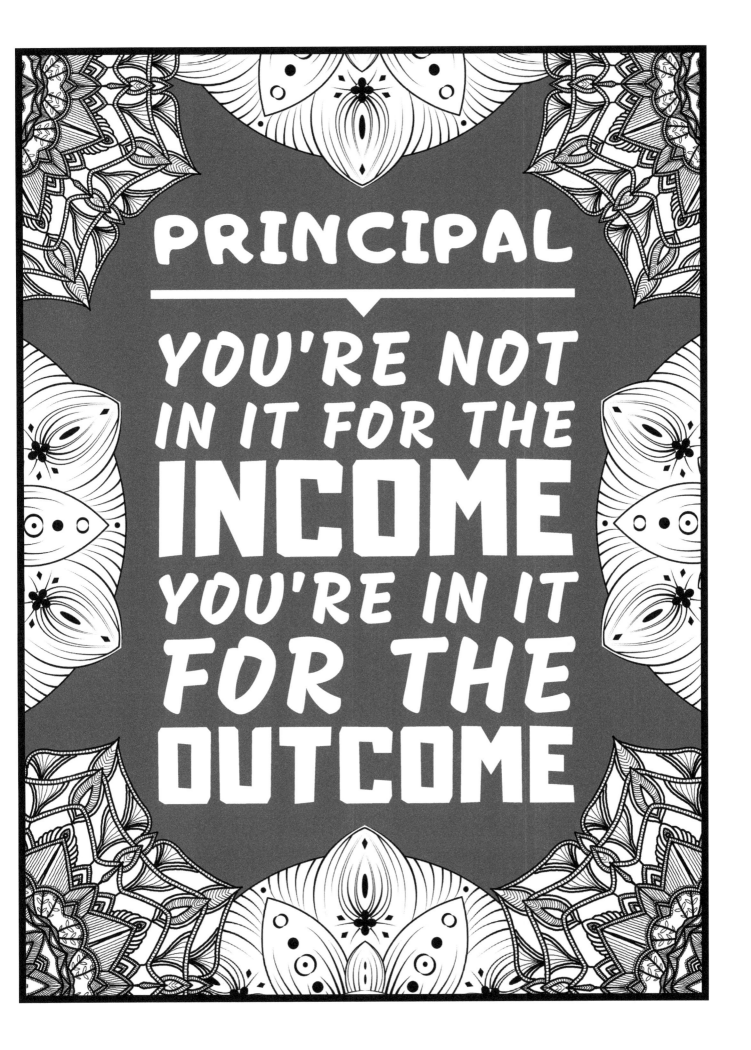

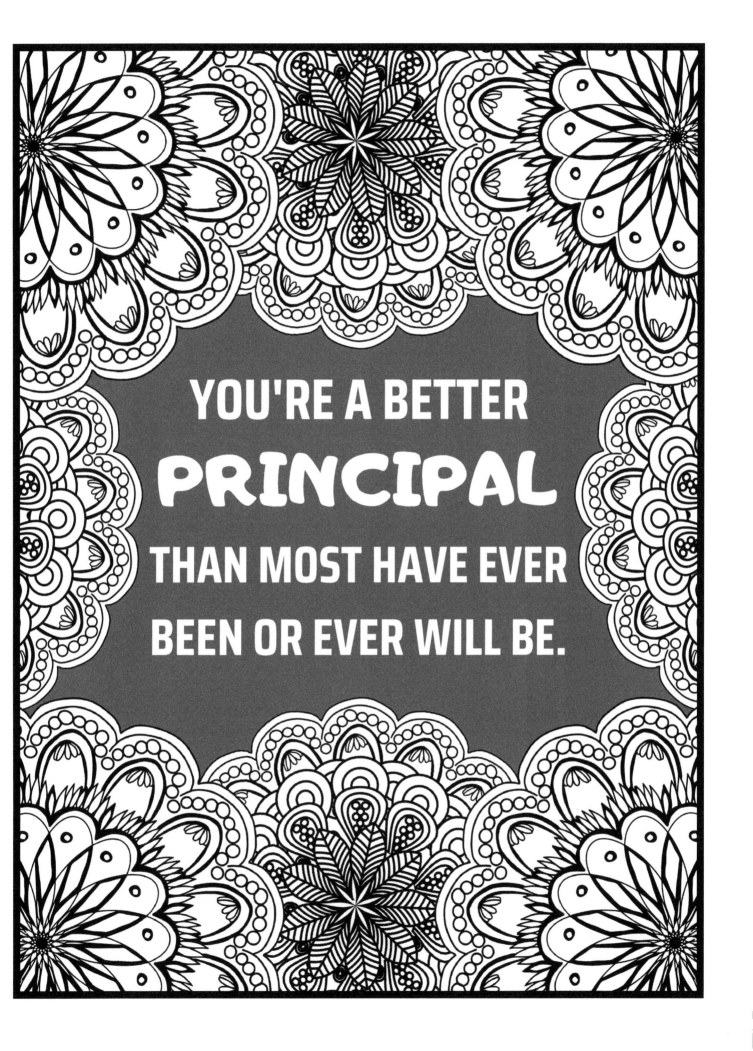

CPSIA information can be obtained
at www.ICGtesting.com
Printed in the USA
LVHW060411020522
717678LV00013B/733